A Tapestry Of Thought
By Antonia B. Laird

Antonia B. Laird

GOLDEN QUILL PRESS
Publishers Since 1902
Manchester Center, Vermont

Library of Congress Catalog
Card Number 95-079006

I.S.B.N. 0-8233-0504-X
Printed in the United States of America

To Ann Lenher Robinson
With affection -
Toni Laird

A Tapestry Of Thought

Other Books
By The Author

A Quiet Voice
A Parasol Of Leaves
A Melody Of Words
Echo Of My Heart
Wings Of Thought
Back Of Beyond
Shadowed Light

To my children, daughters-in-law and grandchildren.
The more the merrier.

Table Of Contents

A Tapestry Of Thought

Lost, One Imagination

Imagination
must be dead,
I haven't heard
his magic words
or seen the shadow
of his shimmering tail.
He must have fled
beneath the sea,
where darkness rims
his coral bed
and holds the brilliance
of his glittering scales.

Spring Dawn

Rise swiftly, dawn,
and chase away the dark,
your soft pink slippers
race away from night
and start the day.
Across the sky
you spread the pastel
panels of your dress,
and in their folds
the birds begin to sing
the early morning
orchestra of spring.

A Late Summer Shower

After the rain
the lake grows calm,
the setting sun
lights up the last
remaining drops
that dress the leaves,
the moss puts on
a fresher face,
and on the higher
Adirondack peaks
the clouds retreat
and vanish
in the evening sky.

Night Sounds

Aches and pains
of an old house,
the walls cry
when the wind blows,
the floors sigh
when the sun sets
and it's dark.

A strange noise
on the wood roof,
sharp claws of
a small beast,
cold stalks
through the house
on its loud feet.

The day comes
with a wide smile,
warmth seeps
through the glass panes,
night ghosts of the
old house
bask in the sun.

Silence Please

Many people seem afraid of silence,
an empty space that has to have a sound.
Television blaring in the bedroom,
loud music played when no one is around.

Men and women often find great pleasure
in talking, yet no one's learned a thing.
After you have silenced all machinery,
tie the tongues that waggle with a string.

An Episcopal Funeral

Funerals always used
to be the same,
hymns, prayers,
the service for the dead,
we shed some tears
for those held dear,
no more was said.
Not now....
A tapestry of thought unfolds
as family, friends, weave stories
that immortalize
the person who has died.
So fine the words
I only wish that she could hear.
Perhaps she does
in some celestial room
that has no doors.

Fall in Virginia

Virginia dresses up for fall,
leaves changing color, green to gold,
brilliant reds adorn the trees,
lovely ladies, bright and bold.

Long after northern leaves have fled,
before harsh winds and talk of snow,
these southern beauties wear a dress
that makes a very splashy show.

No Guarantee

Capture life with nimble fingers,
put him in a gilded cage,
wait to hear the happy trilling
coming from his private stage.
There will be no song, no singing,
'till the day you set him free.
You compose your own libretto,
life comes without a guarantee.

When I Die

Don't say it's a blessing
when I die,
no matter how or why,
I am not blessed
to leave this world behind.
But if my mind
should go before my body
turns to ashes
and I do not know,
please let me die.
There is a time in life
when every spirit
flies away,
and when mine does
I do not want it trapped
in flesh and blood,
but let me fly
above the clouds,
and I will whisper
on a summer wind
one last good-bye.

Solitary Golf

Damp grass
beneath my shoes,
a few high clouds
that open up the day
to sun,
perfection in the sprinklers'
patterned dance.
No need to wait,
to talk,
discuss the game
of golf,
I play alone, reciting verse
I learned by heart
at school.

Bob White, Bob White

"Bob white, bob white"
he softly called,
one morning
right outside my door,
a brown bird
in a feathered coat
who sat alone.
A thin white stripe
above his eye,
a small crest
on a regal head,
"I'm sure you are a Quail"
I said,
"but why alone?"
"My covey is a busy place,
there are a lot of noisy young,
I only sat to rest awhile
outside your door."
I'm sure that's what
he meant to say,
before my new friend
flew away.

Adopt a Pet

I saved the life
of one small gray furred friend,
and been repaid
a thousand purrs
by two green eyes,
soft paws,
and warmth across
my feet at night.
I saved his life,
but as I stroke
beneath his chin
and hear the motor
of his love
beneath my hand,
all worries slip
beneath his fur
and disappear.

Enchanted Sea

A stately galleon sails the sea,
her cabin windows all alight,
a full moon in a velvet sky,
the witching hour of the night.

The ship is bound with silver threads,
a net that shimmers on the mast,
three mermaids swim along its side
and ride the horses of the tide.

"Come sailor boy and share my bed,
a seaweed couch inlaid with pearls,
I'll show you treasures of the deep
and hold you close while we're asleep.

"Beneath the blanket of the sea,
a hidden world for you and me,
I'll let you comb my golden hair,
sing songs of charms I have to share."

Beware young sailor on your watch,
this fish-tailed temptress of the sea,
her kiss will confiscate your breath,
beneath enchantment, only death.

Emily's Paintings

I know it's hard
to let them go,
as finished adults
they must leave the nest
and fly where other eyes and tongues
can spread your fame.
For after all
the moon-kissed witch
who sprinkled
stardust at your birth,
has heard the muse
of painting
call your name.

SeeingThe Barnes Collection

Acoustiguides
don't lecture
with their hands.
Words, not gestures
come at our command
and travel to our ear
when we press "On".
We hear
the lecturer's fine voice
without the blinking
of his eyes
or turning of his head,
no striding up and down.
Instead each picture
comes alive
within this small black box.
So trained
have we become,
that when the music plays
we move along
and leave the Renoirs
glowing in a crowded room.

Old Fashioned Tubs

Old fashioned tubs
had legs and feet,
and squatted
on the bathroom floor
like large white beasts
who had forgotten
how to walk.
A few are left.
Alone they stand
against the glamour
of this age,
when bathrooms
have become the stage
for more
than getting clean,
where tubs wear
any color dress
and whirl their owners
in a porcelain cage.

Glamis House

An old gray house
now turned into a swan,
its face-lift making beauty
out of commonplace.
Not haughty
with a cold veneer,
but warm and open
with a stately grace,
its windows sparkling
in the summer sun.
You stand to greet us
by the door,
a smiling welcome
to your Scotland's shore.

The Red-Bellied Woodpecker

Your loud voice
echoes through the woods,
you tap the trees
in rhythm
with a summer day.
But when the world
is ice and snow,
I know I'll find
you feeding
on my fine seed cake,
dressed stylishly
in black and white,
with quite a handsome
red chapeau.

1994

Guns, knives and drugs
in cities and in towns.
Men gunned down
on busy streets,
while children die
as bullets fly
where they must play.
Women, old and young,
are raped and slaughtered
while the neighbors listen,
all afraid to tell.
A Hell on earth,
where once the criminals
are caught
the lawyers work
to set the bastards free.

Next Time Around

Next time around
my hair will wave,
my fingernails grow long
and never break.
In fluent French
I will converse all night
unless a Spanish diplomat
is on my right.
How Soignée
I will be
next time around.
Every book that's mentioned
I'll have read,
"how brilliant is her bridge"
will soon be said.
Tennis, golf,
they'll fight to partner me,
what a houseguest
I will be
next time around.
Until that time
there's just one thing to do,
without these extra gifts
I'll struggle through,
by being me
and listening to you.

Let's Talk About The Weather

If all our fifty different States
had temperatures the same,
the weatherman would be extinct
without his daily game.
His pretty map would be all green
without a flake of snow,
no tornados down in Texas,
no rivers overflow.
An earthquake wouldn't shake the West,
no ice storms hit the East,
the bitter cold from Canada
would certainly have ceased.
By day a constant eighty-five,
at night a little cool,
if someone said "there is a flood,"
we'd all say "April Fool".
I'm glad there still is weather
as a subject we can trust,
I'd rather talk of ice and snow
than Clinton and his lust.

Thoughts Before A Birthday

Time has fled
so swiftly this past year,
now months and years
all disappear
like footprints
underneath a wave,
hours flee
like minutes did
when we were young.
I'd like to tame
the hands of every clock,
never turn
the calendar's next page,
so I would stay the age
that I am now,
inviting everyone I love
to do the same.

Grief

Grief has tucked herself away
inside a pillowcase of tears,
she sits alone
amidst the sorrow
of a hundred days and nights
that pass as shadowed memories
in an empty space.
No laughing voices
warm the air,
cold winter
never has a spring
when death comes stalking
with a frozen face.

Behind The Smile

You have the most
bewitching grin,
your mouth tilts up
to catch ideas
as they flash by,
then turns them
inside out to make a smile.
You find the best
in everyone,
strong controversies
never were your style,
but when the winning vote
is finally cast,
your smile can lash
a rival to the mast.

Birch Logs

Birch tree, I'd rather see you burn
than made into a lamp or stool,
a border for a mirror on the wall.
Such beauty should be growing tall,
its green leaves whispering to the lake,
not made into a basket or a frame.
Now in my fireplace logs wait,
the match has gone out in my hand,
instead of wood I see the proud birch tree.
Am I a fool to care so much,
all beauty fades when one grows old,
you light the match, the room is getting cold.

The First Snowfall

Night falls
with the quick
twist of his tail,
covers the trees
with a white veil
made with the flakes
from the first harvest
of snow.

Après Ski

I don't like to bake in a sauna
or whirl in a whirlpool bath,
I'd rather swim in the ocean
or walk on a sun-warmed path.

But after a cold day skiing
when the snow has tickled my nose,
I love to lie in a bathtub
and let the heat wrinkle my toes.

After The Storm

On every branch
the snow lies
snug and close,
flung there by blizzard wind
it hugs the trees
and bends them low.
Each tall fir
wears a furbelow
of white,
while Aspens' tangled tops
have stocking caps
to keep them warm
tonight.

A Winter Restaurant

I run a restaurant
for birds.
They fly in feathered flocks
across the sky,
and come to dine
on seeds and grains
with peanuts mixed between.
It's been a winter scene
for months,
snow, sleet and rain.
The chic red Cardinal
chatters to his mate,
while Titmice, Chickadees
and Purple Finch
all push to get their share.

A Winter Sunset

A winter sunset
quivers in the sky.
Between the chill of day
it is a burst of color
chased by night.
It has no time
to dress in fancy clothes,
parade across
a frosty stage.
It disappears
and curtains off the light.

Dragon's Teeth

Dragon's teeth are hanging
from the eaves,
sharp-pointed weapons
made of cold and ice,
they glisten
in the full moonlight
like monster dentures
waiting for a bite.
Next day the afternoon's
warm hands
extract the molars
one by one,
until the monster's
pointed teeth
are pools of water
in the sun.

Two Spruce Grouse

Two Spruce Grouse
resting on the snow
were quite perturbed
when I skied by,
disturbing their cold afternoon.
Without a sound
except the flutter
of their angry wings,
they flew away.
Dear birds
I wish you well,
I have no gun,
and you fly faster
than my skis can run.

Cement Snow

The wind is a cement mixer
tossing the evening snow,
grinding the lightest powder,
flinging it to and fro.

Until when the dawn is breaking,
the trail wears a weighty dress,
I ski through this cement powder,
with my legs in acute distress.

A Perfect Ski Day

The first clear day in ten,
green trees
reach up to frame themselves
against a blue Wyoming sky,
display their eiderdowns
of snow
with great finesse.
How effortless each trail
when you can see.
Instead of feeling
upside down,
you sail across
snow-covered ground
with great vivacity and style,
a perfect day
when even somber
people smile.

Beware The Fisherman

Each day at dawn along the bank,
a fisherman will soon be here
to stand erect on long, thin legs
and wait for breakfast to appear.

It never takes him very long,
in one quick flash a tasty dish,
wide wings outstretched he skims the lake,
beware the Heron, little fish.

Latin Names

Release us,
cry the names
I can't recall,
they've burrowed deep
within the den
I call my brain
and can't get out.
Just yesterday
they flowed across my tongue
like water
down a marathoner's throat,
but now I walk the garden
with a panicked voice
that tries
to conjure up
strange Latin names,
while all the horticulturists
walk on and whisper,
"What a shame."

Tennis Diplomat

I met a diplomat today.
So poised and cool,
I heard him lie
behind his open smile.
In shorts and tennis shoes
and only six,
he had the manners
of a courtly man.
Who else could make
a younger cousin feel
how well she played,
when not one ball of his
had been returned.

Tree Test

Now that summer's song has fled,
each tree has lost its lush green head.
They bow before the snow and rain,
all trees to me now look the same.

I'd hate to have to pass a test
deciding which tree is the best.
Without a single leaf to show,
not one species do I know.

Too Much Flattery

Fake flattery,
a dread disease
that breeds
sweet words,
an endless swirl
of falsehoods
from deceiving lips.
With practice
they become a curse,
or worse,
as in your case
they flow
across a tongue
that has a honey base.
No longer
can you tell the truth.
So many lies.

Youth Is Wasted On The Young

Dame nature plays a dirty trick,
to make you nap, to fall asleep,
when all you want to do is play,
you'll soon be four, your next birthday.

Right after lunch your eyes could close,
how happy you would be to doze,
but now it's work instead of play,
you're forty on your next birthday.

Magnolia Grandiflora

She wears no diamonds in her hair,
no rubies hang around her neck,
but when she blooms,
each large Magnolia blossom opens
in a sea of green,
and soft white petals waft
their fragrance through the air.
A Southern belle
who far outshines
the grandest Yankee in the room.

Survival of the Fittest

A red-tailed hawk
flew overhead,
a gray squirrel
dangling from his bill,
survival of the fittest
in our Chadds Ford world.
Wild predators
who culled the deer
are gone,
as fields and forests disappear
and houses
spring up cheek-by-jowl,
the deer find starving
is a slower way to die,
than hawk and squirrel.

Christmas Night

Candlelight in a dark room
when the table's set for a winter night,
holly placed in a silver bowl,
you on my right.
Fine champagne in a tall glass
while the carols play with a soft refrain,
fleeting magic on Christmas night,
memories remain.

Winter's Bones

When all the leaves
are gone,
the last fall flower cut,
the garden dies
and soon lies desolate
and bare.
When just the evergreens
are dressed,
the other trees'
nude bones must stand alone
in silhouette against
the winter sky.
Their stark gray branches
have a beauty
all their own,
without the ornament
of dress,
until spring's seamstress
starts her leaf machine.

Sore Feet

I never paid them court,
they just were there.
To ski, play tennis,
dance across the floor,
no more,
they hurt!
The doctor says
they'll be just fine,
but in the meantime
I am very cross,
and wonder why
the mermaid
ever wanted feet.

Tigger

The moon
filled with the breath of night,
shines in an August sky,
while the cat,
caught in its path,
polishes his paws.

A New Painting

Drifts of Chadds Ford Bluebells
imprisoned on your brush,
gently scattered
on a river bank.
A dark-veined branch
swept down by wind,
sharp contrast to the blue and green.
A scene now saved
when snow has drifted
close around your house,
the frozen Brandywine
no longer sings.
Above your sideboard
while you dine,
there will be Bluebells
waiting for the spring.

–For "Frolic" Weymouth

Bluebird, Make Up Your Mind

Shy Bluebird perched upon the roof,
looking handsome and aloof,
the time has come, you must decide,
before a Starling flies inside.

I put the house up just for you,
there's nothing more that I can do.
If you want to build a nest
you must fly in before the rest.

The Crabapple Tree

It was her special place.
Tucked in beneath the apple blossoms'
pink perfume,
through green-leafed window
open to the breeze,
she listened
to a spring quartet of birds,
while in her arms
the 'Coon cat
blinked his amber eyes
and rubbed his whiskers
up and down her face.

A Thousand & One Butterfly Plate

Poor butterflies imprisoned on a plate,
a Chinese artist placed you there
to fly a hundred years without a rest.
Each brush stroke blended to the next
to please the foreigner's strange eye.
I wait for one so richly dressed
to reach the freedom of the sky.

The Flower Arranger

One flower seems a little out of scale,
one leaf has just a touch of brown.
I pluck them both, then take a final look,
the lily on the left has fallen down.

The Garden Club will soon be here for lunch.
Snip the stem so it will stay in place,
swear once softly so no one can hear,
then rearrange a rose to fill the space.

The Obituary Page

Age grows calluses
against the death
of friends,
so many tears
have long ago been shed,
the eyes grow dry.
The only question:
who'll be next to die?

The death of someone young
is sad and rare,
it shouldn't happen
to an unlined face
that hasn't felt
the stiff embrace of age,
whose fame should fill
the sports or business news,
and not the cold
obituary page.

Winter's Dessert

Winter
designs her own dessert,
a pile of snow
in a tall tree,
a cold wind
wearing a frozen glove
whipping the froth.

Tea Time

Sleek bombers wearing feathers fill the sky
in "V" formation, waiting for the call to dive.
They circle once,
then plunge their greedy beaks into the sea.
A sudden death as pelicans have fish for tea.

Everything Saved

My mother saved.
I'm sad she died
but mad that we are left
to sort and throw away
her life.
Papers yellowing with age,
old shoes, pocketbooks and gloves,
underwear that's never
left the box,
the list goes on.
I'm in a rage
before the piles of magazines
she saved.
My sisters with more patience
sort and keep,
eighty-seven years of memories
to be read.
When I get home at night
I throw away.
My children will not suffer so
when I am dead.

Sailing into Hellesylt, Norway

Majestic rocks rise up
above the fjord,
their steep sides softened
by a growth of green,
as though a giant hand
had thrown out
a thousand trees
but left the tops quite bare.
They wear a patchwork quilt
of clouds and snow,
while through the mist
the seagulls dip
their black-tipped wings,
and circle high above
the rocks' sharp knees.

An April Wind

A fast express roared by the house,
a jet plane landed on the roof,
has no one told the fool it's spring,
it's time to stop this butchering.

He's crunched the daffodils' green stalks,
snapped off my frangipani tree,
played havoc in my garden bed,
perhaps the poor fool's been misled.

It's April, wind, March days have fled,
it's time to play a different tune,
a waltz instead of rock and roll
to soothe my battered winter soul.

Ann McCoy's Doll House

I stepped inside their magic world
and soon I felt myself grow small,
until the dolls became my friends
and were not porcelain dolls at all.

I took a backward step in time
and found my dress now reached the floor.
My bedroom was a cozy place
with babies filling every space.

I found a lot of work to do,
I cooked a lobster, made a stew.
My favorite friend had brought a cake,
I ate it, what a big mistake!

A bathroom in the latest style,
with Colgate toothpaste by the sink.
A silver service for my tea,
a loving dog beside my knee.

Museum paintings on the wall,
a fine wine for my evening drink,
if only I were really small
I'd never leave their house at all.

Pulmonaria-Blue Lungwort

Medieval ladies used their art
to cure the ills of lungs and heart,
Lungwort soothed a painful throat
when castles still had walls and moats.

Modern gardeners now grow
Pulmonaria in beds for show,
small blossoms changing pink to blue
each year another spring debut.

A Child Forever

When as a child
the thunder crashed,
they told me
giants in the clouds
had bowling balls they rolled
across the sky,
now scientifically explained
are thunder, lightning, fog and rain.
Yet when the heavens
start to roar,
and rumble very late at night,
I still hear giants playing
one last game.

Chateau de Castelngud

Beneath Chateau de Castelngud
the houses cling
like giant snails of stone
whose red tile roofs
stretch out to catch the sun.
A fortress held
for many years by kings,
its battles now
are history in a book.
A peaceful place
where sparrows sing
and circle high above old cannons
that were used in war,
while far below
the Dordogne river
snakes its way
through vine-dressed fields,
pine woods and valleys
garbed for spring.